ALLERGIES

Sarah Lennard-Brown

Raintree
Chicago, Illinois

Copyright Permissions
Raintree
100 N. LaSalle
Suite 1200
Chicago, IL 60602

Printed in Hong Kong

Design: Carole Binding
Photo research: Glass Onion Pictures

**Library of Congress Cataloging-in-
Publication Data:**

Lennard-Brown, Sarah.
  Allergies / Sarah Lennard-Brown.
    v. cm. -- (Health issues)
**Includes bibliographical references and
index.**
**Contents: Allergies and the immune system
-- Allergic illnesses --
Allergens -- Treating allergies -- Living with
allergies.**
  ISBN 0-7398-6421-1 (libr. bdg.)
  1. Allergy--Juvenile literature. [1. Allergy.]
I. Title. II. Series.
  RC585.L385 2004
  616.97--dc21

2003002065

1 2 3 4 5 6 7 8 9 0
LB 08 07 06 05 04

Acknowledgments
The author and publishers thank the following for their permission to reproduce photographs and
illustrations: Cover and pp.1, 11, 12, 18, 41, 42, 57, 59 Topham/ImageWorks; pp.4 (bottom), 46 ZUL,
Chapel Studios; pp.4(top), 10, 20, 27, 31, 50, 55 Science Photo Library: 4t (Damien Lovegrove), 10
(BSIP, Taulin), 20 (Dr P. Marazzi), 27 (Andrew Syred), 31 (J. H. Robinson), 50 (Gusto), 55 (Edoy Gray);
pp.5, 23, 26, 28, 34 Corbis Images: page 5 (Joyce Choo), 23 (Michael Wong), 26 (Gary D. Landsman),
28 (Mug Shots); pp.7, 49 Impact: pages 7 (Peter Arkell), 49 (Simon Shepheard); pp.14, 37, 40, 44,
45, 52 Angela Hampton Family Life Picture Library; p.16 Robert Harding Picture Library; p.24
Topham/Photri; pp.32, 38 Hodder Wayland Picture Library; p.54 Eye Ubiquitous.
The illustrations on pages 8, 15, 19, 43 and 53 are by Carole Binding.

Note: Photographs illustrating the case studies in this book were posed by models.

Contents

Introduction
Do You Have Allergies?

Your chances of developing an allergy depend on your genetic makeup and on your exposure to substances that can cause an allergy. The World Allergy Organization estimates that between 30 and 50 percent of the global population is at risk of developing an allergy. Allergies cause a variety of illnesses that can affect your whole body. The most common allergic illnesses include hay fever (allergic rhinitis), asthma, and sinusitis. The World Health Organization estimates that asthma affects nearly 150 million people, and allergic rhinitis affects more than 115 million people worldwide.

Allergies are uncomfortable and distressing and can also be serious illnesses. Asthma is responsible for approximately 180,000 deaths per year worldwide. Another allergic condition called anaphylaxis is much rarer and can also be fatal; each year about 100 people in the United States die from anaphylaxis caused by food allergies. Allergies are also expensive. The World Allergy Organization estimates that approximately $20 billion is spent globally each year on allergic rhinitis alone. This includes the costs of medication, time off work, and visiting a doctor.

Breathing, eating, and ...
You may be allergic to something that you breathe in, like pollen, or something that you eat, like strawberries.

4

Allergies are sometimes said to be a disease of the modern Western world. Allergies are indeed a growing problem for industrialized countries. It seems that the higher the standard of living, the more likely a person is to suffer from an allergy. This trend is illustrated by the rates of asthma (a common allergic illness) around the world. The highest incidence of asthma is found in Australia and New Zealand; the lowest rates are found in poorer countries and regions such as Albania, China, Eastern Europe, and India.

There are many theories about why there is such a large difference in the numbers of people affected by allergies around the world. People in industrialized nations now spend about 90 percent of their time indoors. Indoor environments are not only comfortable for people but ideal for certain allergens (allergy-causing substances) like molds and dust mites. Another factor may be the poor air quality of industrialized areas. It may even be that our modern standards of cleanliness make us more vulnerable to developing allergies.

... touching
Another way of coming into contact with an allergy-causing substance is by touch, as in the case of detergents.

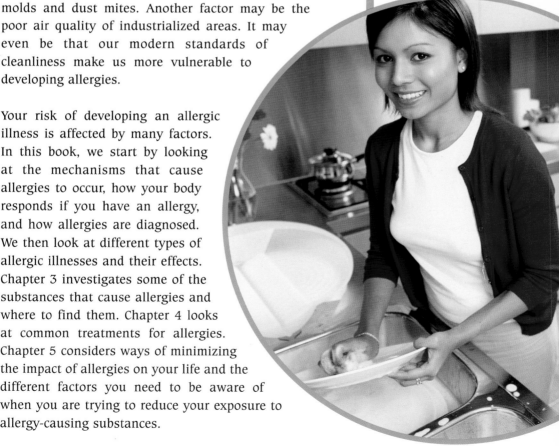

Your risk of developing an allergic illness is affected by many factors. In this book, we start by looking at the mechanisms that cause allergies to occur, how your body responds if you have an allergy, and how allergies are diagnosed. We then look at different types of allergic illnesses and their effects. Chapter 3 investigates some of the substances that cause allergies and where to find them. Chapter 4 looks at common treatments for allergies. Chapter 5 considers ways of minimizing the impact of allergies on your life and the different factors you need to be aware of when you are trying to reduce your exposure to allergy-causing substances.

1 Allergies and the Immune System
Causes and Diagnosis

Having an allergic illness can be very unpleasant. Although allergies rarely cause irreversible damage, they can be a source of constant irritation and discomfort. Allergies occur when your immune system (the system that protects your body from infection) mistakes a harmless substance for something dangerous. Under normal conditions your immune system is very good at telling the difference between harmless substances and things like viruses, bacteria, and parasites that could cause you harm. But when you develop an allergy, your body reacts to harmless substances such as pollen or pet dander as if they were dangerous and produces the symptoms of an allergy.

"I've got this nut allergy thing, you know, one peanut and it's curtains—well almost, I have to get to a hospital pretty quickly. I have to be really careful what I eat."
(Jordan)

Allergies can cause serious problems. They range in severity from allergies to insect stings and some foods, which can be fatal (these are very rare), to asthma, which can be mild or severe, and more minor conditions such as hay fever, which causes discomfort and aggravation during the pollen season.

"I get hay fever in the spring. I sneeze, my eyes run. I hate it. I have to stay indoors as much as possible. Boring."
(Toni)

Inheriting an allergic tendency

Your chances of developing an allergy depend on your genes and your environment. Some people inherit a tendency to develop allergic reactions through their genes. You may find that one member of a family has hay fever, another eczema, and another asthma. Sometimes one individual may be unlucky enough to have more than one condition. This tendency to develop allergies is called atopy, and seems to be caused by slight differences in the gene responsible for the production of a particular antibody called IgE. Antibodies are protein molecules produced by your immune system that are responsible for destroying bacteria, viruses, and parasites.

Inheriting this alteration to the antibody IgE does not necessarily mean that you will develop an allergy. To develop an allergy, you also have to be exposed to something in your environment that stimulates the allergy to occur. This may involve something as simple as coming into contact with a large amount of an allergen. It may also depend on other substances in the environment, such as chemicals or pollution, that make the antibody more likely to react to allergens.

"My mother, uncle, and two of my brothers have allergies. I only get a skin rash when I eat strawberries, so it's fairly easy to avoid it. But one of my brothers has asthma, eczema, and hay fever, so he suffers quite a lot." (Jade)

Unwanted inheritance

A tendency to develop allergies can be inherited. Sometimes several members of one family have allergic illnesses.

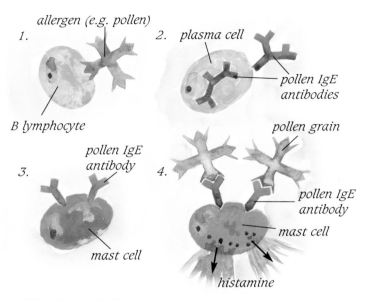

1. allergen (e.g. pollen)

B lymphocyte

2. plasma cell

pollen IgE antibodies

pollen grain

3. pollen IgE antibody

mast cell

4. pollen IgE antibody

mast cell

histamine

Allergic response

1. A B-lymphocyte grabs hold of a pollen grain, which is mistaken for a virus or bacterium.

2. The B-lymphocyte goes to a lymph node and changes into a plasma cell, making large amounts of pollen IgE antibodies.

3. In the bloodstream, the pollen IgE antibodies attach themselves to mast cells. The body is now ready to react.

4. The next time the body comes into contact with the allergen, components of the allergen are detected by the IgE antibodies on the mast cells, which then produce histamine. Histamine causes the allergy symptoms.

Antibodies and allergy

For an allergy to develop, your immune system must become sensitive to the allergen. Two things need to occur. First, your body has to come into contact with an allergen. This can happen when you breathe in a certain substance or eat something, or when something rubs against your skin or is injected into your body (if you are stung by a bee, for example). Second, your immune system must make a mistake and react to the harmless substance as if it were a dangerous bacterium, virus, or parasite.

Lymphocytes (white blood cells) guard your body against infection. They travel around the body looking for bacteria, viruses, and parasites that could cause you harm. When they find a substance that they do not recognize as being part of your body, they react quickly to destroy the "invader." There are two types of lymphocytes, B-lymphocytes and T-lymphocytes. B-lymphocytes are involved in allergic reactions. When a B-lymphocyte finds an unknown particle, it makes a record of the substance and returns to a lymph node, where it changes into a new type of cell called a plasma cell and releases large amounts of antibodies into your bloodstream.

There are several types of antibody, but the antibody particularly associated with allergies is called immunoglobulin E (IgE). When IgE is released into the bloodstream it attaches itself to special cells called mast cells. Your immune system is now sensitive to the substance caught by the B-lymphocytes, and if they have made a mistake and reacted to a normally harmless substance, you have now started to develop an allergy.

Allergic reactions

If you have an allergy, you may experience:

- *Runny or blocked nose*
- *Itchy or watery eyes*
- *Sneezing*
- *Cough*
- *Shortness of breath*
- *Wheezing*
- *Tight feeling across the chest*
- *Skin Rash*
- *Vomiting*
- *Drop in blood pressure*

It can take a week or more for the mast cells to become primed with IgE. However, once you have been sensitized in this way, your body will respond quickly the next time it detects the allergen. Your body will release large amounts of IgE into your system, and your mast cells, now ready for action, will release large amounts of a chemical called histamine into your bloodstream to fight what is considered to be a dangerous invader. It is histamine that causes the symptoms of allergy. It makes your blood vessels expand and leak fluid, and it can also make your airways narrow; a rash (often called hives) may develop, and you may feel your heart beat faster.

How strongly you react to an allergen depends on how much histamine is released by your mast cells and which part of your body is affected. Some allergies caused by things such as bee stings can result in so much histamine being released into the bloodstream that the whole body is affected, and this can be fatal. This type of allergy is called anaphylaxis. Allergies to substances like pollen, dust mites, pet hair, and molds are usually less severe and cause conditions such as asthma, hay fever, perennial rhinitis, and eczema.

Diagnosing allergies

If you visit your doctor with a problem that could be caused by an allergy, he or she will listen to your description of what happens and ask questions such as: How long have you had the problem? Does anything make it better or worse? If the doctor suspects that you have an allergy-related illness, you will probably be prescribed an appropriate treatment or medicine. If this doesn't provide relief, or if your allergy is causing severe problems, you may be sent for tests to try to find out which allergen causes your symptoms. Identifying the cause of your allergy can help you to eliminate it from your environment and can help your doctor prescribe the most effective treatment.

Skin prick testing

Skin prick tests are the most common form of skin tests. They can help doctors discover exactly to which substances a patient is allergic.

Skin tests

These sensitive tests involve contact between a tiny amount of an allergen and your skin. If you have antibodies to the allergen, your skin will react by producing a raised, red, swollen area, which may be itchy. This is called a weal. The larger the weal, the more sensitive you are to the allergen. Skin tests are not appropriate for people suspected of having a severe allergic reaction, because any contact with an allergen can be life-threatening for individuals with these rare forms of allergy. There are four main types of skin test:

● Skin prick test: A number of allergens are dropped onto your skin, at marked positions. The skin under the allergen droplets is then pricked lightly to bring it into closer contact with the allergen. Any reaction is usually visible in 20 minutes.

● Intradermal skin test: More sensitive than skin prick testing, this is sometimes used if skin prick tests have not shown any reaction but an allergy is still suspected. A small quantity of allergen is injected into the top layers of the skin. Any reaction is usually visible in 20 minutes.

● Skin scratch testing: Very similar to the skin prick test, this involves a small scratch being made in the upper layers of skin before the suspected allergen is applied. Any reaction is usually visible within 20 minutes.

● Skin patch tests: These are used to test allergens suspected of causing contact eczema. The allergen is placed on a pad, which is then left on the skin for at least one day. The skin is then observed to see if any of the allergens have caused eczema to occur.

These tests can be very useful in identifying what you are allergic to. However, sometimes the results can be misleading. For instance, a substance that produces a skin reaction may not necessarily produce allergic asthma or hay fever, and substances that cause asthma or hay fever may not produce a skin reaction. Similarly, substances that cause food allergies may not necessarily cause a skin reaction.

Allergic to cats

"I first started wheezing when I was 8 and went to stay with my aunt who bred Persian cats. I loved being there; the cats were beautiful and I helped groom them every day. It wasn't the first time I had been there. I had helped before, and the doctor believes that I must have been sensitized before the wheezing started. It started gradually and just got worse and worse. Mom took me home and the doctor sent me for skin prick tests. I reacted immediately to cat dander. I have to avoid cats and carry an inhaler with me in case I start wheezing."
(Mya, age 16)

Blood tests

Blood tests are sometimes used to confirm skin prick tests or, if the allergy is severe, instead of skin tests, because of the risk of anaphylaxis. Blood tests can measure the amount of the antibody IgE in your bloodstream while your symptoms are at their worst. This can show that an illness is due to allergy rather than another cause.

Occasionally, doctors ask for a blood reaction test, where a small piece of tissue paper coated with an allergen is added to a sample of your blood under a microscope. If the antibodies in your blood are sensitive to the allergen, they will rush to the allergen and start to react with it. Analysis of this reaction can give a good idea of how severe the allergy is and if the individual is at risk of anaphylaxis.

Challenge tests

Challenge tests are usually only done if other tests have given conflicting evidence. They are much less common than skin and blood tests and are only performed in special centers or hospitals, because they carry a small risk of producing an anaphylactic reaction. The tests reproduce the allergic illness under controlled conditions, by bringing the person into contact with a suspected allergen and monitoring the outcome.

Blood testing
Blood tests can show if you have a lot of the allergy antibody IgE in your blood.

● Bronchoprovocation test (bronchial challenge test): After your lung function is checked, you breathe in a small amount of a substance that provokes an asthma attack. Your lung function is checked again to see if your airways have narrowed.

● Nasal challenge test (for allergic rhinitis): You breathe in small amounts of potential allergens and are observed to see if any changes happen.

● Oral challenge test (for food allergies): You are given carefully measured increasing doses of the suspected food and are observed for allergy symptoms.

"I had bad hay fever, and since results from other tests weren't clear I had a nasal challenge test. It turns out that I am allergic to dust mites, not pollen, so staying inside in the pollen season just made things worse!" (Lydia, age 15)

Other allergy tests

Some people claim that they can determine the substances you are allergic to using tests such as hair analysis or kinetic energy analysis. Beware of these tests because there is no evidence that they are able to diagnose allergies. The only reliable tests at the present time are those performed at medically recognized allergy clinics.

Keeping the immune system healthy

The number of people suffering from allergies is growing, particularly in wealthier societies. A study in 1999 found that 38 percent of Americans were affected by an allergy. It is thought that the increase is due to differences in the environment in developed countries. One issue is that of increasing cleanliness. Some people think that our immune system may need to be exposed to regular small doses of dirt and disease in order to give it a workout and keep it healthy. In rich countries, people tend to live in superclean environments and children are less likely to play outside, so their immune systems may not get the challenges they need to develop properly. Undeveloped immune systems are thought to be more likely to make the mistakes that cause allergies. Some researchers are even working to develop microbe vaccines that would exercise our immune systems without making us ill.

2 Allergic Illnesses
Sneezes, Wheezes, and Other Discomforts

There are many different types of allergic illnesses. This chapter describes how they affect people and also looks at some of the factors that increase a person's chances of experiencing such an illness.

Asthma

Asthma is a disease that affects the airways in your lungs. People who have asthma have very sensitive airways, which tend to become inflamed (red and swollen) and narrow. When this happens, it is called an asthma attack. Anything that irritates the airways, making them inflamed and narrow and effectively starting an asthma attack, is called a trigger. Not all asthma is triggered by an allergy. However, allergies to dust mites, animal hair, pollen, and molds are very common asthma triggers, particularly for young people.

A happy bunny?
Allergies to pet dander can trigger asthma.

Asthma attacks

When they become red and swollen, the airways become narrower. This makes it more difficult to get air in and out of the lungs, so the person becomes breathless or short of breath. The person breathes faster in order to get enough oxygen into the body. It takes a lot of effort to get air in and out through narrow airways, and the force needed can result in a whistling noise called a wheeze.

Normal airway *Inflamed airway*

Airways

In an asthma attack, the airways in the lungs become inflamed, making it difficult for air to flow through.

Inflamed areas of the body produce fluid, as part of the immune system response. Inflamed lungs produce fluid called mucus to try to flush out the irritant. This results in the asthma sufferer coughing, as he or she tries to clear the mucus from the lungs to be able to breathe properly. It is very difficult to cough up mucus if your airways are narrow and inflamed. Experiencing an asthma attack can make the person feel frightened and anxious. This fear and anxiety can also cause breathlessness and can cause the airways to close up even more. Asthma attacks can be dangerous; sometimes they can be fatal. So they need prompt medical attention.

Asthma attacks vary in how often they occur, as well as in how bad they are. Some people with asthma experience them only occasionally, but people with severe allergy-induced asthma tend to experience the symptoms regularly. However, a main feature of asthma is that it is reversible: the symptoms disappear once the trigger is removed or once treatment is given. The long-term outlook for people with well-controlled asthma is good. People with allergy-induced asthma usually need to carry properly prescribed medicine, to soothe their airways and open them up, making it easier to breathe.

A growing problem

Asthma is a growing problem for countries around the world. The Global Initiative for Asthma estimates that approximately 150 million people worldwide suffer from asthma. Each year in the United States, more than 5,000 people die from asthma. Asthma also has a substantial cost in time lost at work and school, not to mention the discomfort of asthma itself.

Allergic skin diseases

Allergic skin disease can vary in severity from small, dry, hot, itchy patches of skin to conditions where nearly every skin surface is covered in a scaly, raw, bleeding, itchy rash. Although it can look unpleasant, allergic skin disease is not infectious. It is caused by a reaction to specific allergens.

Allergic skin conditions are a growing problem, particularly in the Western world. In the United States it is estimated that one in nine people have an allergy-related skin condition, resulting in more than seven million visits to health-care providers each year.

Atopic dermatitis (eczema)

Atopic dermatitis, or eczema, is the most common form of dermatitis and affects people of all ages. *Atopic* means that it is caused by an allergic reaction. Common causes include dust mites, pet hair, pollen, and certain foods. Eczema is very itchy, and can be almost unbearable. The skin becomes very dry, red, and inflamed. Intense itching

Eczema
Some eczema is caused by an allergy and it can be very uncomfortable.

leads to scratching, which can lead to the skin splitting and result in infection. Infected eczema can crack and weep, or slowly leak a clear fluid.

Atopic eczema commonly affects infants and children. In the United States, about 9 percent of the population is affected by atopic eczema. Most (but not all) people find that their eczema gradually improves as they get older. Two-thirds of children with eczema find that it has virtually disappeared by the time they reach their mid-teens. There are other forms of eczema that look like atopic eczema, but are not caused by an allergic reaction.

"I had bad eczema as a child. I remember the itching even now. But what I remember most is other children not wanting to touch me because they thought—wrongly—that they could catch something."
(Toby)

Allergic contact dermatitis

This skin condition occurs when an allergy develops to a substance that is in contact with your skin. It is commonly linked to nickel, which is often found in costume jewelery, buttons, and buckles. It can also be caused by an allergy to perfume or latex (rubber). At the point of contact with the allergen, your skin may become itchy, red, and swollen, and small, fluid-filled blisters may appear. These often break and dry out to leave crusts and scales. Eventually the skin may darken and become leathery.

Urticaria (hives)

Urticaria, or hives, is a red, itchy rash, with no blisters. This can be caused by a variety of things, including allergens. The rash can appear with more serious allergy problems, such as anaphylaxis, but it can also occur as a mild allergic response to things like eating strawberries or eggs. Health-care workers may get urticaria from an allergy to latex gloves. Urticaria can also occur as the first sign of an allergy to medicines.

"I developed an allergy to the metal in my watch. It was horrible. My skin got all red and scaly. It was so embarrassing. It went away eventually, after I stopped wearing the watch."
(Alison, age 17)

Allergic rhinitis (hay fever)

Allergic rhinitis causes sneezing, itchy and watery eyes, runny nose, and tiredness. It can be caused by an allergic reaction to several allergens, particularly pollens but also dust mites, pet hair, or molds. Allergic rhinitis that only occurs at specific times of year is usually caused by pollen or molds. Problems that occur year round (sometimes called perennial rhinitis) may be caused by a pet-hair or dust-mite allergy. Allergic rhinitis isn't usually a serious condition, but it can cause misery and prolonged suffering for people affected by it.

Allergic rhinitis usually develops before a person reaches the age of 20. Once you have developed the condition, it does not mean that you will have it for the rest of your life. Symptoms of allergic rhinitis caused by pollen allergy tend to be worst during a person's mid-twenties and then gradually diminish as he or she gets older. Most people will have very few symptoms of allergic rhinitis by the time they are in their forties.

Approximately 26 million Americans (10 percent of the population) are thought to suffer from allergic rhinitis. Its estimated cost to the United States in 1990 was over $1.8 billion. This includes the cost of health care and time off of work.

Not just spring
The sneezing and itchy, watery eyes associated with hay fever (allergic rhinitis) can occur at any time of year.

Frontal sinuses

Ethmoid sinuses

Maxillary sinuses

Frontal sinus

Sphenoid sinus

Allergic sinusitis

Allergic sinusitis involves inflammation of the linings of the sinuses. These are cavities that connect to your nose and throat, and they help to moisten and warm the air you breathe in on its journey to your lungs. Allergic sinusitis produces a clear, watery discharge from your nose, which can run down the back of your throat and cause coughing. Your nose may feel blocked and itchy. Your ears may also feel itchy as a result of allergic sinusitis. You may sneeze

The sinuses

Sinuses are cavities located in the bones of your face and forehead. They help warm and moisten the air that you breathe in.

Understanding the problem

"We see many people with allergic sinus and allergic rhinitis conditions, and these seem to us to be getting more common. We see the most cases in spring and early summer, when the pollen count is high. We are a rural practice, inland, away from sea breezes, and we have quite a lot of grassland around us. We probably see more people with these allergic conditions than, say, a practice near the coast, because of the geography of our area and the types of plants that grow here. People can be dismissive of the importance of these conditions because they are so common, but it is important to take them seriously; they cause a lot of suffering, and not just in spring and summer. Many people suffer all year round, due to allergies to dust mites and molds."
(Lionel, family doctor)

repeatedly and your eyes may water and itch. Common allergens that cause allergic sinusitis include pollen, pet hair, feathers, and molds.

Having allergic sinusitis makes you more likely to develop an infection in your sinuses, and this can lead to chronic sinusitis, where the symptoms persist or worsen over many weeks or months. Chronic sinusitis is the most common chronic disease. In 1996, it was estimated to affect 12.6 percent of the United States population (about 38 million people) and to cost approximately $5.8 billion in health-care expenses.

Allergic conjunctivitis

Allergic conjunctivitis is the name given to allergic reactions affecting the inner eyelid surfaces and membranes at the front of the eye called the cornea and conjunctiva. Both eyes are usually affected at the same time, and you may experience intense itching, redness, and inflammation of the tissues inside the eyelid. This form of allergic disorder usually occurs with allergic rhinitis or allergic sinusitis. It is often associated with sensitivity to dust mite droppings, pollen, and pet dander.

Allergic conjunctivitis
When you have allergic conjunctivitis, both eyes become itchy, swollen, and red.

Food allergies

True food allergies are very rare. They can produce quite severe reactions in people who are susceptible to them. These reactions include swelling in the body (sometimes called edema), swelling in the throat, urticaria (rash), vomiting, stomach cramps, diarrhea, and, in the most serious cases, anaphylaxis (see page 22). Food-related anaphylaxis is often associated with specific foods and occurs immediately or soon after the food is eaten. The food can cause a reaction even if it is present in minute amounts. This is particularly the case with nut allergies.

Rarely, food allergies can be connected to other allergic illnesses, such as allergic rhinitis and asthma. However, the symptoms then may not occur until several hours after the food has been eaten, and quite large amounts of the food need to be eaten for a reaction to occur.

Food allergies are most common in small children and babies whose immune systems are immature and therefore more likely to make the chemical mistake that causes them to react to a harmless substance. Most food allergies tend to improve as people get older and their immune system matures. However, people with the most severe forms of food allergy, including allergies to peanuts, eggs, and shellfish, tend to have their allergy throughout their lives.

In the United States, food allergies are thought to affect approximately 8 percent of children under 6 years old and 1 to 2 percent of adults, and cause approximately 100 deaths per year. About three million Americans have allergies to peanuts, or other nuts.

"I'm allergic to milk. It's so annoying. I have to be really careful that I don't eat anything that has dairy products in it."
(Ashley, age 15)

Food intolerance or food allergy?

There is an ongoing debate about the relationship between food allergies and food intolerance. Many people think that these two conditions are the same thing. They are not. Food allergy involves an adverse immune reaction to a particular

Common allergens
Peanuts, tree nuts, wheat, soy, eggs, shellfish, fish, and dairy products are the most common allergens in food allergies.

food, and when severe, it can be life threatening. Food intolerance involves an adverse reaction to food, which does not necessarily involve the immune system. Food intolerance can cause problems such as bloating, indigestion, tiredness, general aches and pains, headaches, diarrhea, and constipation. It cannot cause anaphylaxis (see below) and is not life threatening. Only a true allergy, which involves an immune system response, has the potential to cause an anaphylactic reaction.

"I thought I was allergic to milk, but my doctor found that I wasn't. Apparently, I just have trouble digesting it. I'm not allergic to it. I am seeing a dietician now about changing my diet."
(Leyla, age 14)

If you experience any unpleasant symptoms that you think may be related to a food you have eaten, you need to get checked out by a doctor. The symptoms that should concern you are: rash, swelling, wheezing, or shortness of breath. Food allergies can be very serious, and occasionally fatal, so they need to be taken seriously.

Anaphylactic shock

Anaphylaxis is the name given to the most severe form of allergic reaction. It is very rare and usually only a problem for people who are allergic to certain foods (such as milk, peanuts, shellfish, eggs, and nuts), insect stings, latex (found in products such as rubber gloves and balloons), or some medicines (particularly those given by injection, in large doses). People most at risk of an anaphylactic reaction include those who have had an anaphylactic reaction before and people who have multiple allergies, especially those who have asthma as well as food allergies.

In susceptible people, anaphylaxis can happen as soon as five minutes after being exposed to the allergy-causing substance. Most cases begin within an hour of exposure, though in some cases it can take two to four hours. Anaphylaxis involves a whole-body response to an allergen. People may find that their skin starts itching and a red rash may erupt over their body. Their lips may tingle and swell, and they may become hoarse and start to wheeze. Muscle cramping may occur. They get a sensation of tightness across the chest, and they may feel short of breath. They may also feel confused or anxious. Sometimes they faint. If not treated promptly, anaphylaxis can be fatal.

If someone does have a severe allergic reaction, it is important to get the person medical help as quickly as possible. Often people who have this sort of severe allergy carry an injection of adrenalin with them. Adrenalin reverses the symptoms of anaphylaxis very quickly.

Some people may appear to recover from an anaphylactic reaction, and then the reaction returns two to three hours later. This form of response is called biphasic and can be particularly dangerous because it takes the victim by surprise.

Peanut panic

"My friend Abe has a peanut allergy. I didn't think anything of it till he collapsed when we were at the park. Abe had a hot dog and the guy in the kiosk had been eating peanut butter sandwiches, then touched the hot dog. I've never seen anything like it! Abe's lips got swollen and he got this rash, and then he sat down suddenly, holding his chest. His brother rushed up and stuck what looked like a pen in Abe's leg. It was an adrenalin injection. He came around and they took him to the hospital. I was sure glad his brother was there. I didn't have a clue what to do."
(Darius, age 15)

Why allergic illnesses do or don't develop

The tendency to develop allergies is to some extent inherited through our genes. However, other factors also play a large part in determining whether you go on to develop allergic illnesses. These include the environment you live in, how many allergens you are exposed to, levels of stress, general health, and whether you were breast-fed as a child.

Breast-feeding

Breast feeding has been found to reduce the likelihood of a child developing an allergic disease, especially if it is continued for the first year of life. Babies do not receive just nutrients from breast milk but also antibodies, and this protects them from illness and helps their own immune systems to develop properly. Breast milk is easier for babies to digest than cow's milk or soy milk. Also, the proteins in cow's milk and soy milk can produce allergies in children who are susceptible to them.

Breast milk
The antibodies and nutrients naturally present in breast milk help a baby's immune system to develop properly.

However, a mother breast-feeding a baby who is susceptible to allergic illnesses may have to be very careful what she eats, because there is some evidence that peanut allergens can be transmitted through breast milk to the baby. This would mean that a baby could become allergic to peanuts even if the baby's only exposure to peanuts was through the mother's eating them. This sort of sensitivity is thought to be very rare.

Viral infections

Viral infections including colds and flu are usually spread by coughing and sneezing. Coughs and sneezes distribute live viruses into the air, which you may breathe in if you are unlucky enough to be nearby. The viruses settle in your airways and multiply, irritating the airways and making you sneeze and cough so that you send more viruses out to infect other people. Your immune system notices it has an unwelcome visitor (or a few thousand) and sets to work to eradicate them before they can do major harm.

Any infection makes your immune system work harder. When your immune system is working hard, it is more likely to make a mistake that leads to an allergy developing. When your body is under stress (for example, from an illness), allergies tend to get more severe and you can become more sensitive to allergens. How this process works is unclear, but new research may help uncover the mechanisms behind it.

"My eczema gets much worse when I have a cold. It improves when I'm healthy." (Anya, age 16)

Stress and anxiety

Strong emotions can have an effect on allergies. The link between feelings and health is very complex. Stress has been demonstrated to reduce the effectiveness of your immune system. For people who are at risk of allergies, this can mean that their immune system is even more likely to make the mistake that causes an allergy to develop. So experiencing a stressful event such as the breakup of a relationship can reduce the effectiveness of your immune system and make it more likely that you will become ill or develop an allergy.

Environmental factors

High levels of air pollution make you more likely to develop allergies if you are genetically susceptible to them. Also, if you have an allergic illness, air pollution can make your symptoms worse because it irritates areas that are already inflamed.

No smoking

Cigarette smoke is a common airborne pollutant that can make allergic illnesses worse. A baby born into a smoker's family is far more likely to develop allergies than a baby born into a nonsmoking family.

3 Allergens
Where They Are Found

Allergens are substances present in the environment that can cause an allergic response. An allergy occurs when a genetically susceptible person is exposed to a large enough quantity of allergen in their environment to provoke the development of an allergic reaction. The amount of allergen required to produce an allergic response depends on the individual and how sensitive he or she is. Many substances are potential allergens, and most of them occur naturally in the environment; very few are human-made.

Dust mites

Dust mites are one of the most common allergens. These microscopic creatures (distant relatives of the spider) love our modern standards of living. They flourish in warm, humid conditions and live on the skin cells that we shed every day. The mites themselves do not cause allergies; it is their droppings that cause the problem. A dust mite produces up to 20 dung pellets a day. The pellets contain partly digested skin cells (their favorite food) and enzymes, wrapped in a protein covering. (The enzymes continue to break down the remaining skin cells so that the mites can eat them again later and get some more

Allergens at home
Allergens can be present in high levels in warm, humid, unventilated homes.

nourishment from them.) It is the dung covering that is the main allergen.

Dust mites do not drink, but they contain up to 80 percent water. This means that they need a humid, moist environment to survive. Dust mites live happily in warm (not too hot and not too cold), moist, unventilated homes: in bedding and soft furnishings, curtains, carpets, cushions, soft toys, and anywhere that is dusty. There are millions of them even in the cleanest homes.

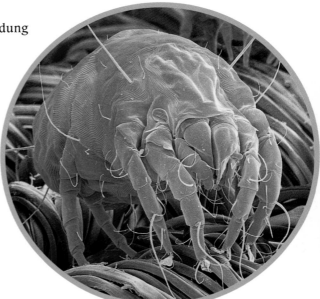

Cockroaches

People who are allergic to dust mite droppings may also be sensitive to cockroach allergens (see page 33). Cockroach scales, eggs, saliva, and droppings are all potent allergens, which are also found in house dust. Cockroaches eat almost anything, but their main food sources are waste food, paint, wallpaper paste, and book bindings. Cockroaches also need water, warmth, and a place to live (cracks and crevices). Cockroaches are a big problem in many countries around the world, particularly those with warmer climates. Many children with asthma also have cockroach allergies. Children who live in crowded apartment buildings are at a greater risk of developing both conditions.

Dust mite

Dust mites are found in dust and in the soft furnishings of even the cleanest home. This colored electron micrograph shows a dust mite on some fabric fibers.

Pet hair and feathers

Pets are a common source of allergens. It is possible to develop allergies to hair, skin scales (dander), saliva, urine, and feces of animals. Any home with a pet will be full of these particles, especially in soft furnishings. It is difficult to get rid of these allergens. Dander from pets can still cause a problem up to six months after the pet has left the house. A study published in June 2001 found that more than 330,000 cases of asthma in children could be directly related to having a pet in the household.

Medicines

Medicines are important tools for fighting disease and only rarely cause allergies. However, the reactions can be severe. Some people can have anaphylactic reactions to some medications. If you are sensitive to certain medicines, it is important that everyone involved in your medical care be aware of this. Most allergies to medication first show when a rash develops after taking the drug. People with asthma may find that they have an asthma attack after taking a medicine. Any reaction of this sort should be reported to your doctor immediately.

Some medicines are more likely to cause an allergic response than others. These include penicillin, aspirin, nonsteroidal anti-inflammatory drugs, and any drug that is given intravenously (directly into a vein) and in large doses.

Household chemicals

Many common household cleaners contain chemicals called volatile organic compounds, which can trigger allergies. These chemicals are made from petroleum oil and can cause irritation to eyes, nose, lungs, and skin as well as allergic reactions. Other products that contain these chemicals and can trigger allergies include air fresheners, paints, glues, varnishes, and some aerosol sprays.

Researching detergents

"We have to be aware of the potential of the new detergents we are working on to cause allergies. Many of them are irritants that can cause skin problems in nonallergic people. People should always wear gloves when using household cleaning products. I myself have asthma and I have to be very careful to take precautions when I am working with cleaning products."
(Ling, chemist researching new detergents)

Natural gas and kerosene

The gases given off by natural gas and kerosene heaters are not allergens, but they do increase the potency of other allergens. It is thought that the gas binds to the allergen particles and makes it more likely that the immune system will react to the particle and start an allergy. One study found that cooking with kerosene increased the risk of developing an allergic illness by 78 percent.

Food

It is possible to be allergic to any food, but up to 90 percent of all food allergies are caused by eight groups: milk, eggs, soy, wheat, peanuts, tree nuts, (for instance, cashews, hazelnuts, walnuts), shellfish, and fish. Food allergies can cause a range of allergic problems, such as hives, rhinitis, asthma, and eczema. They can also be responsible for the most severe form of allergic response, anaphylaxis.

Peanuts are the food most commonly linked with anaphylaxis (though other food allergies can also result in anaphylaxis). For a person who has an anaphylactic response to a food, even the tiniest trace of the food can induce the response. For people with peanut sensitivity, this can mean that they have to be careful about eating any foods that have been produced in a factory or kitchen where peanuts have been used, even if the foods themselves do not contain peanut products. It can also mean being aware of the contents of cosmetics. Arachis oil, which is derived from peanuts, has excellent skin-softening properties and, in the past, was frequently used in cosmetics. People with severe forms of food allergies must keep emergency treatments with them (see page 42).

Nut allergies
Peanuts are a well-known cause of food allergies, but tree nuts such as cashews, Brazil nuts, and walnuts can have the same effects.

Molds

Mold spores can trigger an allergic reaction in some people, causing perennial rhinitis or asthma. Molds are an essential part of the ecosystem; they help to break down plant and animal material into vital nutrients needed by other plants. Mold spores, like seeds from a plant, enable the molds to reproduce themselves. They are released into the air, usually during late summer and fall, a time when you often see their fruiting bodies: fungi and mushrooms. However, molds that grow indoors can release their spores at any time of year.

Mold spores can be found in warm or cool moist places, indoors or outside. Well-insulated, warm houses are prime breeding grounds for molds. They thrive on windows that gather condensation, in damp areas around sinks, in bathrooms, and in damp walls and roofs. Molds also live in the compost around potted plants. Their spores often collect in house dust.

Pollen

Pollen is a powerful allergen and is linked to several allergic illnesses, particularly perennial rhinitis and asthma. There are many varieties of pollen. Some people are sensitive to just one and will experience more allergic symptoms when that particular pollen is in the air. Others are sensitive to several different pollens and their symptoms will be more long-lasting. Some pollens are more likely to cause an allergic response than others. Grass pollens are particularly bad, as is the

Pollen timetable
Different types of plants produce pollen at different times of the year. If you have hay fever, you can sometimes determine which pollens you are sensitive to by keeping a record of when your symptoms are worst.

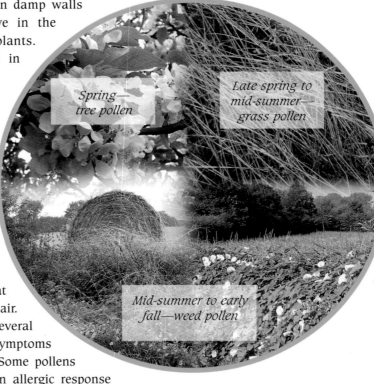

Spring— tree pollen

Late spring to mid-summer— grass pollen

Mid-summer to early fall—weed pollen

pollen ragweed. Ragweed grows in many areas of the United States. Pollen from ragweed is most prevalent from August to October, which is often called "ragweed season."

Pollen is a powerful allergen. Some studies suggest that children born during the pollen season are more likely to develop asthma. However, there is no evidence that children born on farms, where more pollen is present, have more cases of asthma.

Stinging insects

Allergies to insect stings can be very dangerous. This form of allergy causes at least 40 deaths per year in the United States and affects approximately 3.3 percent of the population. The most common stinging insects found in the United States include wasps, honeybees, hornets, yellow jackets, and fire ants.

"When I get stung by a wasp, I get bad swelling and feel terrible. Antihistamines help. I carry them with me in the wasp season."
(Toby, age 17)

The most common allergic reaction to insect stings involves swelling of the area stung, larger than the site of the sting. For example, if you are stung on the foot, an allergic reaction might cause your whole foot—or even your leg and foot—to swell. You may also experience a fever and feel sick. If someone is severely allergic to insect stings, anaphylaxis can happen within minutes of receiving the sting. It is essential that people susceptible to this form of allergy carry emergency medication with them.

Wasp stings
Some people are allergic to insect stings. These allergies can cause severe swelling and sometimes anaphylaxis.

Allergens in the workplace

Working environments often bring us into contact with potential allergens. These can cause allergies to develop in people who are susceptible to them but have never had any symptoms before. Allergies caused by allergens in the workplace are called occupational allergies. The majority of occupational allergies cause asthma or dermatitis (skin allergy).

"I developed an allergy to the hair dye chemicals we use. We were supposed to wear gloves to prevent this, but sometimes I didn't. I wish I had listened now."
(Denise, hair stylist)

Trying to find the cause of an occupational allergy can be tricky. One study found that, of an estimated six million chemicals in the environment, approximately 2,800 could be classified as allergenic. Some substances in the workplace are well-known allergens. These include:

- Isocyanates, which are chemicals often used in spray-painting, adhesives, foams, paints, and plastics
- Fumes from soldering and welding, processes often used in the electronics industry
- Chemicals found in some floor cleaners
- Dust, especially from grains (including flour), wood dust (especially hardwoods and western red cedar), and latex dust
- Latex

Surgical gloves

Health-care workers who become allergic to latex gloves need to use surgical gloves that do not contain this substance.

Latex

Latex is produced from the sap of the *Hevea Brasiliensis* tree and has been used extensively in manufacturing, particularly for making tires, balloons, tubing, flooring, shoes, and surgical rubber gloves. It is an extremely useful substance, but, unfortunately, it is also a particularly potent allergen. Latex allergy can cause eye problems, sneezing and coughing, hives, and occasionally anaphylaxis. In the

United States, latex is responsible for approximately 220 cases of anaphylaxis and 3 deaths per year.

Latex allergies are a particular problem for the following workers:

- Health-care workers who wear latex gloves
- Food handlers who wear latex gloves
- Workers in manufacturing industries using latex products

Latex allergies and spina bifida

Latex allergies are a particular issue for people with spina bifida, a condition that occurs when the spinal bones do not form properly when a baby is developing in the womb. It now seems that up to 78 percent of people with spina bifida may have latex allergy. Why this should be is not clear, but one theory is that people with spina bifida have constant exposure to latex products from a very early age, through surgery, diagnostic tests, and various other medical procedures, and that this might increase their susceptibility to the allergy.

However, latex allergies are not only confined to the workplace because rubber products are everywhere. Latex is even used in the coatings of glossy paper. Latex can be found in elasticized clothing, footwear, rubber bands, toys, diapers, and magazines; the list is huge. Sufferers from a latex allergy can also be at risk from food that has been packed by people wearing latex gloves.

Cross-reactivity

Sometimes an allergic reaction is caused by a substance that is chemically very similar to the allergen that first provoked the allergy. This is called cross-reactivity and is an important issue for people who suffer from allergies. Substances that are similar in their chemical construction do not necessarily look or taste alike, and so some unexpected, unrelated things might trigger the usual allergic response. For example, people with latex allergies may have cross-reactivity allergies to bananas, avocados, and chestnuts, because proteins in these foods are very similar in chemical structure to the latex protein. Similarly, people with an allergy to dust mites may show cross-reactivity to storage mites, bird feathers, egg yolks, and shrimp proteins.

4 Treating Allergies
Soothing and Preventive Medicines

Treating asthma

Treatment for asthma involves reducing exposure to asthma allergens and regularly taking the medication prescribed by the doctor. People with asthma often require more than one type of treatment and so their doctor will put together a treatment plan that is right for the individual person.

Relief Medications

Relief medications are usually prescribed as inhalers, although there are also some reliever pills. Inhalers are a form of medicine that you breathe directly into your airways so that it starts to work immediately at the site of the problem. The medicines work by making the muscles relax around the inflamed, narrow airways. This enables the airways to open further, making it easier to breathe.

Inhalers
The inhaler in this picture is being used with a spacer. Spacers enable the medicine to be breathed in effectively so none of it is lost.

Preventive Medicines

Preventive medications are also usually taken as inhalers. They work by soothing the lining of the airways. They reduce inflammation and make the airways less sensitive to allergens. When you take them properly, you are less likely to experience a severe asthma attack. For preventive medicines to work effectively, you have to take them every day, even if you feel well, and it can take up to fourteen days for them to start taking effect.

"The inhalers help as long as I take them regularly."
(Isabella, age 15)

Inhaled steroids are one main type of asthma preventive. They are very effective for allergic forms of asthma. The steroids mimic chemicals that are naturally produced in the body and that soothe inflammation and irritation. Inhaling the steroid medicine takes it straight to the inflamed airways, which means that only tiny amounts are needed and there are few side effects.

"I've had asthma since I was small. It's better than it used to be. I try not to let it rule my life."
(Simeon, age 16)

Another type of preventive inhaler is called a mast cell stabilizer or inhibitor. Mast cells are part of the immune system (see page 8). Once sensitized, they react to the presence of allergens by releasing the chemical histamine into your bloodstream. Mast cell stabilizer medicines calm down the mast cells and stop them from being so active. This reduces the inflammation in the airways and makes them less sensitive to any allergens breathed in.

Some other preventive medicines are antileukotrines. These are taken as pills. Leukotrines are chemicals found in the muscles around your airways and in the lining of your lungs. They make these muscles irritable (twitchy) and cause them to grow larger. Antileukotrine medication works against this process, making it easier to breathe. Antileukotrines are a new component of asthma treatment and are becoming increasingly popular.

Antibiotics

People with asthma are at a higher than normal risk of developing chest infections. Antibiotics are an effective treatment for chest infections caused by bacteria.

Some people may have an allergic reaction to an antibiotic, particularly penicillin, and develop an itchy rash and swelling around the face and lips. If this happens to you, you should stop taking the antibiotic and contact your doctor for advice.

Steroid pills

For people with asthma whose symptoms get worse, doctors may prescribe steroid pills. Steroid pills are a much stronger dose than a steroid inhaler and are very effective at reducing airway inflammation. Usually they only need to be taken for three to fourteen days.

Treating allergic rhinitis (including hay fever)

As with most allergies, allergic rhinitis is treated by both avoiding the allergen and taking medication to relieve the symptoms. The three main medication are antihistamines, decongestants, and preventives.

Antihistamines

Histamines are chemicals that are produced by the immune system and cause inflammation. Antihistamines are medicines that stop the inflammation process. They can be taken as pills, nasal sprays, or eye drops to relieve the symptoms of allergy at the point where they are most irritating.

Antihistamines are available over the counter at pharmacies, and qualified pharmacists are able to give information about which type is most appropriate. However, it is essential that you are careful about the mixture of medication you are taking for your allergies. Taking more than one type of medication, for example, an antihistamine with certain cough medicines, can cause dangerous side effects. Medical advice should always be sought before taking combinations of medicines, to ensure that they do not interact badly.

"The antihistamine I used to take for hay fever made me feel really sleepy. Then Mom talked to the pharmacist and found one that helps stop my eyes from watering but doesn't make me sleepy. Much better!"
(Harry, age 12)

Decongestants

Decongestants reduce the symptoms of nasal congestion that often accompany rhinitis problems. They must be used for only a few days at a time. If used for longer, they can lose their effectiveness and cause rebound nasal congestion when they are stopped. As with antihistamines, it's wise to ask the pharmacist about which would be suitable and how to use the treatment.

Preventive treatment

Preventive medicines for allergic rhinitis include mast cell stabilizers (see page 35) and steroids, which are also useful for reducing irritation. The amount of steroid needed to act as a preventive for allergic rhinitis is so small that there are rarely any side effects associated with its use. These preventives are usually given in the form of nasal sprays, nose drops, or eye drops.

If these forms of treatment provide only limited relief, your doctor may suggest desensitization (see page 40).

Treating allergic sinusitis

Treatment for allergic sinusitis is very similar to that for allergic rhinitis. It is based on avoiding the allergens that produce symptoms, and treating any symptoms that do occur with antihistamines and preventive medication such as mast cell stabilizers and steroids. You may also need to take medication to relieve the pain caused by congested sinuses. Your doctor may recommend that you use saline (salty water) nasal spray or rinses to reduce the feeling of pressure from blocked sinuses.

Treating allergic conjunctivitis

Treatment for allergic conjunctivitis also involves the use of antihistamines, mast cell stabilizers, and steroids, in order to reduce the symptoms of allergy. For eye conditions, though, these are usually applied as eye drops, ointment, or cream. For certain types of allergic conjunctivitis, especially a variety called atopic keratoconjunctivitis, which also affects the eyelid, cold compresses can help relieve the intense itching and swelling.

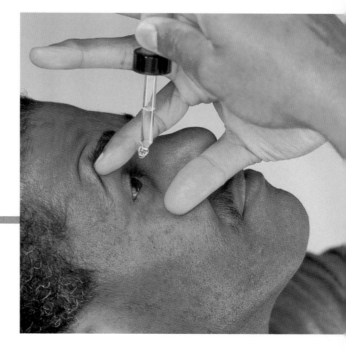

Eye relief
Antihistamine treatment can relieve the discomfort of allergic conjunctivitis.

Treating eczema and allergic contact dermatitis

There are several treatments for eczema and allergic contact dermatitis that can be very effective when they are used as part of a regimen that also involves avoiding allergens.

Emollients

Emollients are creams that reduce water loss from the skin and prevent dermatitis and the itch associated with dry skin. The emollients provide a barrier between the skin and anything that might irritate it. They come in various forms: ointment, cream, and lotion. Once dermatitis occurs, emollients may not be strong enough to treat it. The emollients may also further irritate the skin.

Steroid creams

Doctors sometimes prescribe steroid creams to treat eczema and allergic contact dermatitis that is very inflamed and uncomfortable. Steroid creams lessen the inflammation and irritation of a skin rash and can help the

Applying cream
You need to wash your hands after applying steroid creams to prevent them from coming into contact with your eyes or your mouth.

healing process by reducing the production of histamine (see pages 8–9). Steroid creams come in many different strengths, and your doctor will prescribe the lowest dose necessary to help relieve your skin condition. Steroid creams are applied in a very thin layer to the affected area. It is important to use as little as possible, because the medication is strong.

Other treatments

Other treatments for allergic skin conditions include antihistamine tablets or creams, ultraviolet light treatment (usually only used for severe eczema), and wet-wrap bandaging to reduce itching. It can also help to keep cool, especially at night, and to make sure that fingernails are kept short to reduce the damage done by scratching. Sometimes it is recommended that children wear cotton mittens at night to stop them from scratching in their sleep.

"My daughter had eczema as a baby. We used to have to put mittens on her at night to stop her from scratching herself."
(Jean)

Treating urticaria

Antihistamines are the main medication used to treat urticaria. They can help relieve any itchiness accompanying the rash and help the rash to gradually get better. If the condition does not improve, a doctor may prescribe steroid creams or (rarely) steroid pills. Allergic urticaria usually disappears within a few days if you avoid the allergen that causes the rash to occur.

If you get hives after you have eaten something or been stung by an insect, then it is important that you visit your doctor. It can be a sign that you are developing a serious allergy that may result in anaphylaxis.

Steroid pills

Very occasionally, with severe allergic skin conditions, it may be necessary to take steroid pills. Again, the doctor will prescribe the lowest dose possible. If steroid pills are taken for a long time, there is a risk of side effects. These include slowed growth (mainly a problem for children who are still growing), developing a round (moon) face, weight gain (due to an increase in appetite), bruising, and osteoporosis (bone thinning).

People who take steroids need to carry a steroid card with them, so that if they have an accident the doctor treating them will know they are on steroids and need to keep taking them. Steroids are very powerful and their use needs to be reduced slowly.

Treating food allergies

The only effective treatments for food allergies are an exclusion diet (excluding the allergens that cause your symptoms) and, sometimes, desensitization. However, the latter is usually considered too dangerous for people at risk of anaphylaxis.

You should always consult a doctor before starting an exclusion diet, because it is vital to ensure that you still get all the nutrients you need. It can also be very difficult to follow such a diet. We eat many convenience foods and packaged foods, and there may be allergens hidden in the ingredients of all of these. People with food allergies have to become experts at reading food labels. (The issue of avoiding food allergens is covered in more detail in chapter 5.)

The risk of cross-contamination is a problem, too. Cafés, restaurants, and food-processing plants deal with many different foods, and it is impossible to guarantee that traces of one food are not carried on to another. Such cross-contamination could be very serious. For some people it takes only a few molecules of a food substance to set off an allergic reaction. People at risk of an anaphylactic reaction to a food allergy should carry an emergency adrenalin injection with them, in case they come across the food allergen unexpectedly.

Food awareness
People with food allergies have to read the list of ingredients on each package very carefully to make sure that they avoid the foods they are allergic to.

Desensitization

If you have an allergy, it may be possible to have desensitization treatment at an allergy clinic. This involves being given a series of injections over several months.

The treatment begins with skin prick testing (see page 10), to confirm what you are allergic to (the allergen). This is followed by a series of tiny injections containing minute amounts of the allergen. The injections may be continued for a long time; depending on the individual, they can be given over a period of several months up to five years. The aim of the injections is to retrain your immune system not to react to the allergen. It is important to try to avoid the allergen while you are having the desensitization injections.

Desensitization can be very effective at reducing the severity of allergy-induced illness and, if you react well to the treatment, improvement in symptoms can last for several years after finishing the injection course. There is a small possibility of having an anaphylactic reaction to desensitization injections. Therefore, a competent medical practitioner with emergency equipment available should always perform the treatments. This means it is usually best to have the treatment in a hospital or clinic.

Working at the allergy clinic

"I work in an allergy clinic attached to our local hospital. We see a large number of people every day with various allergies. Desensitization is one of the treatments we use. For example, if you had severe hay fever and it affected your school work or stopped you from working, your doctor may decide that desensitization would be an appropriate treatment. It doesn't take long to come in and have the injections, but you do have to come in regularly for many months. We have to be sure that people are going to keep coming, since the treatments are expensive and, if you miss a few, then you might as well not have had any. For people who do have the whole course it seems to be pretty effective. I'd say that the majority of patients here find their symptoms improve."
(Andrew, allergy clinic nurse)

Emergency treatment for asthma

Occasionally, someone with asthma may have a severe asthma attack that does not respond to the relief medicine they keep with them. If an asthma attack does not improve after a dose of relief medicine, you should contact your doctor or call an ambulance (or get someone to do this for you) and keep taking the medicine every few minutes until the ambulance arrives or until the doctor directs you to do otherwise.

In the hospital you may be given some oxygen to help your breathing. You may also be given an atomizer with a high dose of relief medication. An atomizer is a machine that pumps air through a solution of medicine and saline in order to create a fine mist. You may be given steroids, and, if you have a chest infection you may also be given antibiotics. You may need to stay in the hospital until your asthma is under control again.

Emergency treatment for anaphylaxis

Anaphylaxis can happen within five minutes of being exposed to an allergen. The reaction involves the whole body: an itchy, red rash may develop; lips may tingle and swell; the throat may become swollen so that the voice becomes hoarse; breathing becomes difficult so the person may wheeze; muscle cramps may occur; and the person feels dizzy, confused, and anxious.

Emergency injection

People who are at risk of anaphylaxis often carry emergency injections of adrenalin with them.

If someone develops an anaphylactic reaction, it is essential that he or she have an emergency injection of adrenalin. If the person has an emergency shot available, it should be used immediately. It is also vital to get the person to a hospital as quickly as possible so that he or she can be given an

Anaphylaxis first aid

If someone is having an anaphylactic reaction:

1. *Remind him to use his emergency epinephrine shot.*
2. *Call an ambulance. It is important to get to a hospital as quickly as possible.*
3. *Keep her sitting up, since this makes breathing easier.*
4. *Reassure him and keep him calm.*
5. *Do not give her anything to eat or drink.*
6. *If he carries an inhaler, he may take a puff.*
7. *If she becomes drowsy or unconscious, put her in the recovery position.*
8. *Keep a careful watch on his breathing and pulse. Be prepared to use mouth-to-mouth resuscitation if necessary.*

adrenalin injection, and so that his or her essential body systems can be supported if the reaction continues.

Adrenalin (also called epinephrine) is a natural hormone produced by the body. It reverses the anaphylactic reaction by increasing blood pressure and reducing swelling. People known to be at risk of anaphylactic reactions usually carry a dose of adrenalin with them, in the form of a "pen" or automatic injector. It is essential to get an injection of adrenalin as soon as the symptoms of anaphylaxis start; the sooner it is given, the less likely the reaction will be severe.

Anaphylaxis can be fatal, so if you are at risk, it is essential to carry an adrenalin shot with you. You never know when you might come across an allergen. It is also wise to wear a Medicalert® bracelet or necklace that gives details of your condition, and to make sure that the people you are with know what symptoms to look out for and what to do in an emergency.

Recovery position

This is the safest position for someone who is unconscious, while waiting for emergency help. Ensure that the chin is up, to keep the airway open so that the person can breathe.

Complementary therapies

No complementary therapy can cure allergies, but some therapies can help people manage them better and reduce their symptoms. If you want to try a complementary therapy, do not stop taking your prescribed medicine and let your doctor know before you begin. This is important, because some complementary medicines can be harmful for people with allergies.

"I've tried everything, but the only thing that makes any difference is the antihistamine my doctor prescribed."
(Aiden, age 19)

Exercise

Exercise-based therapies, such as yoga, Pilates, tai chi, and martial arts, can all have a beneficial effect on allergic asthma symptoms. This is because they increase your general fitness level and they all involve breathing exercises, which can help you stay in control during an asthma attack. Another potential benefit from these exercise therapies is that they involve learning to relax. This can be useful in preventing asthma attacks from becoming severe, by helping to keep you calm and relaxed when an attack occurs.

Acupuncture

Acupuncture involves the insertion of very thin needles at points on your body, based on Chinese theories of natural energy paths. Some research into the benefit of acupuncture for people with asthma and allergic rhinitis has shown that it can be helpful in the short term. Acupuncture does not normally produce side effects. However, it is wise to make sure that you are seeing a properly qualified practitioner who is using sterile acupuncture needles.

Pilates training
Exercise classes help improve your fitness and your breathing technique, and this can help you stay in control during an asthma attack.

Homeopathy

A homeopathist makes a detailed assessment of a person's problem and character and then treats the problem with tablets containing a very tiny amount of a substance that would produce similar symptoms if taken in large doses. Homeopathy can be helpful if you know what you are allergic to. Some researchers have claimed that some people with allergies can be helped by homeopathy—particularly by a form of treatment called homeopathic immunotherapy. However, more research is needed to prove the value of this treatment.

Royal jelly and propolis

These products can provoke a severe allergic reaction in people who are allergic to pollen.

Complementary medicines

These include herbal medicine, Chinese herbal medicine, and homeopathy. Some herbal medicines have been shown to help reduce asthma symptoms. Those that may be helpful include ginkgo biloba, tylophora asthmatica, coleus forskholii, and saiboku-to. However, some herbal medicines can be harmful, and you should always get your doctor's advice before taking a herbal preparation.

Some products from bees, particularly royal jelly and propolis, which are commonly sold as medicinal products, can be very dangerous for people with allergies. They can provoke a severe allergic reaction. It is wise to avoid any products containing royal jelly and propolis if you have a history of asthma, or allergies to pollen.

"Homeopathy was really helpful. When I took the remedy correctly, my symptoms were a lot better."
(Nicole, age 18)

The medicines and treatments described in this chapter are one part of preventing allergic illnesses and relieving their symptoms. The second component of managing allergies successfully involves reducing your exposure to allergens.

5 Living with Allergies
Risk Reduction and Being Prepared

Just as important as taking the correct medication is identifying what you are allergic to and reducing your exposure to it. This can be harder than it sounds. If you are unsure what causes your allergy, and skin prick tests are not an option, one way to try to find out is by keeping a diary or record of your allergy symptoms and your contact with the common allergens. You may find that a pattern emerges. For example, your symptoms may be worse in the morning and improve during the day. This might indicate that you are sensitive to something in your bedroom, perhaps dust mites. You could then take action to reduce your exposure and see if there is an improvement in your symptoms.

Reducing dust mite difficulties

The rise in the number of people across the world who suffer from allergies is closely associated with rising wealth and standards of living. In today's soft-furnished, centrally-heated, well-insulated buildings, people are exposed to more allergens than at any time in history. One of the main allergens that increase greatly under these conditions are dust mite droppings. Dust mites live on dead skin cells, which we shed every day. They like a warm, moist environment to live and breed in.

At home
Lots of soft furnishings, combined with central heating and poor ventilation, can cause a large buildup of dust mites.

Here are some tips for reducing the number of dust mites in your home.

- If you can afford to, replace old, worn mattresses, pillows, and covers.
- Consider buying dust mite–proof covers for your mattress and pillows.
- Change your sheets regularly (weekly, if possible) and wash the sheets at a high temperature setting.
- Make sure your bed is properly aired every day. Turn back the covers over the end of the bed and leave the bottom sheet open to the light and air for a few hours. Because dust mites cannot drink, they rely on a humid, dark environment to stay alive.
- Wash soft toys and then put them in a plastic bag in the freezer for a few hours. Cold temperatures kill dust mites.
- Cushions and pillows also benefit from a regular stay in the freezer (if you have one large enough).
- Use a vacuum cleaner with a special filter, and damp-dust regularly. (Some people who are very sensitive to dust mites need to do this every day.)
- Reduce the number of soft furnishings in your home. Use blinds instead of curtains. Replace carpets with hard flooring such as linoleum or wood.
- Make sure that any soft furnishings remaining are vacuumed and cleaned regularly.
- Make sure there is adequate ventilation. Open windows and air out your home daily, if possible.

"My allergic rhinitis has improved a lot since we started getting rid of dust mites."
(Rosa, age 15)

"If my room is not dusted and vacuumed every day, my asthma gets worse."
(Anka, age 13)

Avoiding food allergens

If you have a food allergy, you may try to avoid the allergen responsible by excluding it from your diet. However, you should consult your doctor about following such a diet, because completely excluding one food source can be bad for your health. You need to ensure that you get all the nutrients required for good health and growth. If your doctor suspects that you have a food allergy, she or he may suggest that you talk to a dietician, who can help you make sure that you eat a balanced diet and keep as healthy as possible.

"I once kissed a guy who had been eating peanuts. Anaphylaxis can be a very disappointing way to finish an evening."
(Katlyn, age 18)

Food allergens can be very difficult to avoid. You have to learn to read the labels on packaged food very carefully, because the same food substance can appear with different names on different packages. The following lists show some of the issues that people with food allergies need to bear in mind.

Milk allergies
- Stores often use the same surfaces and implements for serving dairy as they do other delicatessen products.
- Restaurants often put butter on steaks to add flavor.
- Some processed meats contain milk products.
- Some brands of canned tuna contain milk products.
- "Casein" on food labels means that the food contains milk products.

Egg allergies
- Some vaccinations are grown in egg embryos and therefore may cause an allergic reaction. The person should check with his or her doctor before having any vaccinations.
- Some egg substitutes contain real egg white.
- Many pasta products contain egg.
- Egg is used to create a foam topping on some drinks such as coffee or milkshakes.

Peanut and other nut allergies

- Arachis oil is peanut oil.
- Chocolate may be processed in factories that also process nuts.
- Products from bakeries are often made in areas where nuts are used.
- Sunflower seeds are often processed in equipment that is also used to process nuts.
- Breakfast cereals are often processed in factories that process nuts.
- Some natural or artificial flavorings may be derived from nuts.
- Nuts may be one of the ingredients in products such as sauces, cereals, crackers, cookies, and ice cream, so labels need to be checked very carefully.
- Bean bags, cushions, and soft toys are sometimes filled with crushed nut shells.

Hard to choose
Choosing what to eat can be especially difficult for someone who needs to avoid food allergens.

Fish allergies

- It is wise for someone allergic to one species of fish to avoid all species because of the risk of cross-reactivity (see page 33).
- Seafood restaurants or restaurants serving fish should be avoided because of the risk of cross-contamination.
- Fish protein can be present in the air, so fishing docks and markets selling fish products should all be avoided.
- Caesar salad dressing and Worcestershire sauce often contain fish paste.
- Imitation crab meat is often made with fish.

Soy allergies

- Soybean products are used in the majority of processed foods around the world and especially in the United States.

- Soybean products are particularly found in bread and baked goods, canned tuna, cereal, crackers, cookies, sauces, soups, and sometimes peanut butter.

Wheat allergies

- Many processed foods contain wheat products. Food labels should be read very carefully.

- Some types of imitation crabmeat contain wheat, as do most soy sauces.

Removing animal allergens

The allergens produced by furry and feathered pets are particularly hard to get rid of. If you have an allergy to animals, it is best not to have them at home at all. If you cannot live without them, make sure that they do not go into your bedroom and main living areas. You can also reduce the amount of dander produced by your pets by giving them a weekly bath, keeping them outside as much as possible, and washing your hands after touching them. It is possible to remove pet allergens from your home by steam cleaning, but this is fairly drastic and expensive.

If you decide not to keep your pet, then don't be surprised if your allergy symptoms do not improve immediately. It can take up to six months for pet hair and dander to disappear from a home completely.

Cockroaches

Some people become allergic to cockroach saliva, shells, droppings, or egg cases.

Keeping cockroaches at bay

The cockroach parts that are most likely to cause allergic reactions are their droppings, egg cases, saliva, and outer coverings. Allergy to cockroaches can be severe and can cause anaphylaxis.

As big as mice

"I developed an allergy to cockroaches from an apartment. It was in an old building from the 1960s. It was damp and there was trash everywhere—no one looked after it—and the cockroaches! I swear that some of them were as big as mice. I've never seen anything like it. It was disgusting. I started to get a runny nose and itchy eyes and eventually found out that I was allergic to cockroaches. But you couldn't get away from them in that dump. They were everywhere. We moved as soon as possible."
(Morgan, age 16)

It is important to avoid cockroaches as much as possible. Cockroaches need food, water, warmth, and a place to hide in order to survive. To prevent them from breeding in your home:

- Do not leave food out. Store it in airtight containers.
- Keep work surfaces, sinks, tables, and floors clean. Clear all food crumbs and spilled food immediately.
- Wash dishes as soon as you have finished with them.
- Do not leave trash lying around indoors. Put it in containers with tight-fitting lids, and empty these daily into an outside can. Keep newspapers, boxes, and other trash outside, in sealed containers.
- Fix any plumbing leaks or damp areas quickly.
- If you suspect a cockroach infestation, get professional help in dealing with it.

Taking care with household cleaners

Household cleaners contain a cocktail of chemicals, some of which can act as allergens and some of which are irritants and can produce symptoms very similar to an allergy, such as skin rashes and wheezing. Common chemicals in cleaning products that can become allergens include ammonia, chlorine, chloroform, isocyanates, isopropanol, perfume, and solvents. To avoid contact with these chemicals, always wear waterproof gloves when using them. Also, remember that there are alternatives to modern household cleaners that are not as likely to cause an allergic reaction. These include:

- Vinegar mixed with water for cleaning windows (newspaper is also good to use as a "cloth" for cleaning windows)
- Baking soda disolved in warm water for cleaning sinks, refrigerators, and freezers

Choose cleaning products and washing powders labeled "hypoallergenic." This means "not likely to act as an allergen."

Getting rid of household molds

Well-insulated, warm, humid homes are an ideal breeding ground for molds. They thrive on windows where condensation gathers, usually in kitchens and bathrooms. They also grow in damp plaster, wood, and houseplant soil. For people who are allergic to molds, the household kind are particularly troublesome because they release spores (the main allergen) throughout the year. The conditions loved by molds are the same as those enjoyed by dust mites, so many of the strategies to get rid of one of the problems also get rid of the other. To avoid or get rid of household molds:

Mopping up
Condensation on windows is a prime breeding ground for molds. The condensation needs to be removed every morning to prevent mold from growing.

- Shut the bathroom door and open a window or use an exhaust fan when running a bath or having a shower.
- Replace shower curtains regularly.
- Dry damp towels as quickly as possible.
- Dry clothes outdoors as much as possible, and make sure that electric clothes dryers are vented outside.
- Don't use potpourri, which can provide a growing surface for mold.

- Open windows each day so air flows through the home.
- Mop up condensation from windows daily.
- Clean the rubber gasket around the refrigerator and freezer doors, removing the black mold growth.
- Cut down on houseplants and regularly replace the top layer of soil where molds grow.

Checking your cooking fuel

Using natural gas or kerosene for cooking can raise the level of nitrogen dioxide in your home and can result in increased sensitivity to allergens so that your allergy symptoms are more severe. Exposure to nitrogen dioxide is reduced if you keep kitchen windows and doors open while cooking and keep doors to the rest of the home shut. If you have severe allergies, it may be worth changing to another cooking method, such as electricity. Gas-fired central heating is not such a problem because it is vented outside.

Managing a latex allergy

Latex allergies are difficult to manage, because you need to avoid a long list of products that contain latex. Around the home, for example, latex is found in elastic bands, clothing that contains elastic (for instance, socks and some sportswear), ice cube trays, diapers, baby pacifiers and bottles, balls, balloons, bicycle tires, and some decorating and art products. It is important to read the label of any product that is flexible or stretchy or that may contain latex. Look for alternatives that contain silicone, plastic, or vinyl.

It is also advisable to wear a Medicalert® bracelet or necklace. Medical procedures often involve products made with latex, such as medical gloves, bandages, tape, catheters, intravenous tubing, and tourniquets (used when taking blood). If the doctor or hospital knows that you are allergic to latex, they can use alternative equipment that is safe for you.

Medicalert

Medicalert members wear a bracelet or necklace engraved with their allergy or illness, a personal ID number, and the Medicalert phone number. In an emergency, doctors can contact Medicalert for complete medical information about members that may affect their treatment.

PHONE (555) 555-1234
ALLERGIC: LATEX
Back

MEDIC ALERT
Front

Stinging insects: reducing your risk

An allergy to insect stings can be very serious; however, this type of allergy is rare. Anaphylactic reactions to insect stings occur in less than 5 percent of the people who are allergic to them.

Any insect sting that causes a skin reaction bigger than 4 in (10 cm) across should be reported to your doctor because you may be developing a sting allergy. If you are allergic to insect stings, you can do several things to minimize your chances of being stung:

- Use insect repellents both outside and inside during summer months, when stings are more likely.
- Don't wear clothing that attracts insects. This includes black, flowery, or brightly colored clothing and shiny surfaces.
- Wear shoes to avoid being stung if you accidentally step on a stinging insect.
- Wear long sleeves and pants.

Insect attractant
Avoid wearing brightly colored, loose clothing and eating sweet things outside if you are allergic to insect stings.

Molds outside the home

Molds outside are a vital part of the ecosystem, helping to break down organic matter and providing nutrients for other living things. They are commonly found in woods, compost heaps, and trash cans—anywhere there is dead plant or animal material. These molds tend to produce spores in warm, moist conditions, so spring and fall are more likely to be problematic for people allergic to molds. Barns used for storing hay and grain are best avoided if you suffer from such an allergy.

- Avoid loose clothes; close-fitting clothing makes it less likely that an insect will be trapped in the folds.
- Avoid strong perfumes and cosmetics with powerful fragrances.
- Avoid eating or drinking sweet things outside.
- Don't panic if you see an insect. Swatting at it and panicking make stings more likely. Keep still if a stinging insect lands on you; it will fly away soon on its own.

Taking pollen precautions

If you have a pollen allergy, it will be worse at certain times of the year. Pollen is very hard to avoid because it blows for many miles. Some areas have a higher pollen count (a measure of the amount of pollen in the air) than others. In general, the pollen count tends to be less on the coasts because ocean breezes blow the pollen away. Regular reports on the current pollen count are published in local newspapers, on the Internet, and on television and radio as a guide for when people should take more care.

- Wear sunglasses to prevent pollen from irritating your eyes.
- Shower and wash your hair every evening to remove any pollen grains that have attached themselves to you.
- Cover your bedclothes with a bedspread or sheet during the day to prevent pollen grains from getting on your pillow.
- Damp-dust daily to remove pollen grains that have gotten into the home.
- Vacuum daily using a bag that will filter out particles as small as pollen grains.

Pollen grains
This colored electron micrograph shows pollen grains (pink) and dust (blue) on the surface of someone's trachea, or windpipe.

- Keep windows closed as much as possible during the pollen season.
- Keep pets outside as much as possible during the pollen season.
- Get someone else to mow the lawn and stay inside while it is being done.
- Avoid going out when pollen counts are high. Levels are highest early in the morning, early evening, on windy days, and during thunderstorms.
- If you are severely affected, consider buying high-powered air filters that remove pollen grains from the air.

"One of the advantages of being allergic to pollen is that you get out of mowing the lawn."
(Jason, age 12)

Allergies at work and school

Many working environments involve substances that are potential allergens. If people's allergy symptoms are worse at work and improve when they are away from the workplace, they may have occupational allergies. It can take many years for an occupational allergy to develop.

There is a great deal of legislation relating to the way allergenic substances are used in the workplace. In many countries, employers are obliged by law to ensure that workers are protected from exposure to allergens. Action to protect people from allergens at work can include installing proper ventilation, supplying equipment to prevent workers from being exposed to an allergen, and replacing an allergenic substance with an alternative. For example, if a worker's allergy is triggered by latex and the job involves wearing latex gloves, then the employer would be obligated to supply gloves made from a different substance.

At school there are many substances that can act as allergens. Schools are usually covered by the same health and safety legislation that applies to working environments. If you are sensitive to a substance found at school—for example, wood shavings, chemical fumes, fur

School blues
Classes outside in the spring are not much fun if you have an allergy to pollen.

and feathers in biology, or chemicals used in art classes— you need to let your teacher know. The school health and safety representative or medical personnel should be able to suggest alternatives to the substance you are sensitive to or ways of avoiding it.

Allergies can cause problems beyond just their symptoms for people at work and at school. If you suffer from an allergy, you may feel unwell and tired. This can result in days off sick and not performing at your best. Some people with allergies find that their school grades suffer. It is wise to let teachers and employers know about the problem, to reduce your exposure to allergens, and to take appropriate medication to minimize the impact of your allergy.

"Allergies can be very difficult for some students to manage. Those with hay fever can find it really difficult to last through exam time."
(Astrid, school nurse)

Allergies and vacations

Vacations can be a mixed blessing for people with allergies. Some vacation destinations can be fantastic, especially if you are allergic to substances found in your normal home environment. The vacation gives you a break from unpleasant allergy symptoms. On the other hand, a vacation can be problematic if you go to a place that increases your exposure to the substances you are allergic to. For example, if you are allergic to pet hair and go to a home that has had pets in it, then you may feel worse than you did at home. If you are allergic to pollen and go to a rural location during the pollen season, you could have a miserable time.

On vacation there is also the danger of coming across allergens unexpectedly. When you are in a new or unfamiliar environment, it can be far more difficult than it is at home to keep aware of the foods you are eating or the substances you come into contact with. For example, it may be more difficult to find out whether the food you are offered has been prepared in a place where nuts have been present.

Learning from experience

"I have bad eczema. I am allergic to perfumes and some detergents. It is very difficult for me if I come into contact with these things, because I get covered in a gross rash that does not look pretty. It mostly affects my arms, but once, on vacation, I walked across the swimming pool floor with bare feet and I got eczema on the soles of my feet. They had been cleaning the floor, using a detergent I am allergic to. It was not nice. Now I wear shoes in the swimming pool. The eczema is horrible, but now that I know what causes it, it is easier to avoid. The doctor has given me a special cream. When the rash is bad, I wear long sleeves so no one can see it. It is better than it used to be."
(Stephanie, age 16)

These difficulties should not make you avoid vacations altogether. The important thing is to be well prepared. Make sure that people are aware of your allergy and the need to avoid the substances that cause problems. (This is particularly important for people with food, sting, and latex allergies.) Always carry essential medication with you and ensure that you are prepared for emergencies. Be aware of situations that may bring you into contact with the substance that causes your allergy. Then, knowing that you are prepared in these ways, you can relax and enjoy yourself!

Allergies are, at best, unpleasant and uncomfortable. However, with sensible management and planning, it is possible to minimize the discomfort and live a happy, normal life.

Well-planned break

Good vacation planning is essential for people with allergies. Plan for the worst and then relax and enjoy the activities and adventure.

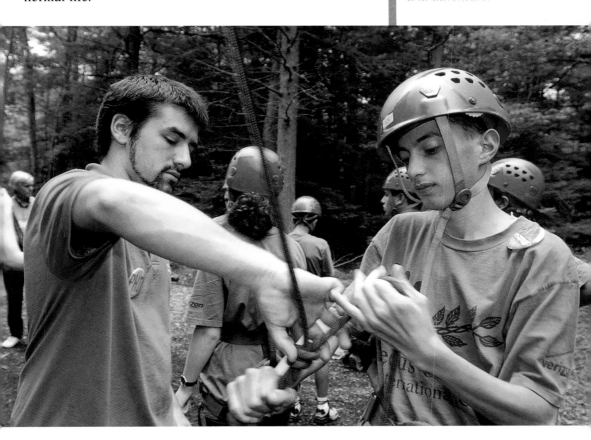

Glossary

adrenalin — naturally occurring hormone that helps the body respond to stressful situations. It is used as a medicine to combat the effects of a severe allergic reaction.

allergen — substance that causes an allergy

allergy — problem that occurs when the immune system reacts to a harmless substance as if it were a dangerous virus, bacterium, or parasite

anaphylaxis — serious whole-body shock condition that can result from a severe allergic reaction

antibodies — protein molecules produced by the immune system that circulate around the body, neutralizing bacteria and viruses

antihistamine — medicine used to treat a mild to moderate allergic reaction

asthma — disease that affects the airways in the lungs. The airways become inflamed and narrow, and this makes breathing difficult. Asthma is usually caused by an allergy.

atomizer — piece of equipment that produces a mist of air. It is used to deliver medicine to the lungs.

atopy — genetic condition that means you are susceptible to developing allergies

bacteria — very small single-cell organisms that can cause disease

complementary therapy — treatment used in addition to standard medical treatment, often to help patients feel good about themselves or to reduce pain

conjunctivitis — inflammation of the tissues surrounding the eye

damp dusting — dusting using a slightly dampened cloth. The moisture on the cloth traps the dust and prevents it from flying into the air.

dander — dead skin cells and feather scales that are shed by animals; the animal equivalent of human dandruff

decongestant — medicine that works to reduce the thickness of mucus produced in the nose and sinuses

dermatitis — red and inflamed patches of skin caused by allergy or irritation

desensitization — action taken to make the body less sensitive to a substance, so reducing the severity of an allergy

diagnosis — doctor's expert opinion about the name of the disease that is causing the patient's problems

eczema — red, scaly, itchy rash

emollient — softening and soothing substance applied to the skin

gene — part of the genetic code present in each of the body's cells. The genetic code controls the way the body grows and develops. It is inherited from parents.

genetically inherited — passed from parents to children through genes. Characteristics such as eye and hair color are passed on in this way.

hay fever — allergic condition in which pollen irritates the lining of the nose and causes sneezing and mucus production

histamine — chemical released in response to infection, allergy, or injury, which results in inflammation

hives — *see* urticaria

homeopathy — treatment that involves giving a person small amounts of a substance that, in larger doses, would produce similar symptoms to those caused by the illness

IgE — immunoglobulin E, the antibody involved in allergies

immune system — body's defense system. It searches out and destroys viruses and bacteria, protecting the body from infection.

inhaler — device that allows medication to be inhaled into the lungs where its effect is needed

intradermal — into the top layers of the skin

irritant — substance that causes inflammation when it comes into contact with the body

lymph node — small organ in the lymph system that is involved in the immune response

lymphocyte — type of white blood cell that can produce antibodies

mast cell — cell that produces histamine when stimulated by an antibody

mucus — fluid produced by the lungs and other mucous membranes in the body. When lungs are healthy, the mucus there is clear. With a chest infection, mucus may become thick or runny, green or yellow

nonsteroidal anti-inflam-matory drug — medicine that reduces inflammation and does not contain steroids

parasite — organism that lives in or on another organism. In humans, these include tapeworms, threadworms, and head lice.

penicillin — antibiotic medicine

perennial rhinitis — constant inflammation in the nose, often caused by an allergy

sinusitis — inflammation of the sinuses

spore — reproductive agent of molds and fungi

steroid — drug that mimics the action of hormones, the body's natural steroids. Steroids are often used to reduce inflammation and swelling.

urticaria — redness of the skin accompanied by small, flat, raised red spots

virus — infective agent that, once it gets inside a cell, reproduces and rapidly infects other cells. Viruses are responsible for many illnesses including the common cold, flu, and chicken pox.

weal — white or pinkish raised area of skin

Resources

Organizations

American Academy of Allergy Asthma and Immunology
611 East Wells Street
Milwaukee, WI 53202
www.aaaai.org

American Lung Association
61 Broadway
6th Floor
New York, NY 10006
www.lungusa.org/asthma

Asthma and Allergy Foundation of America
1233 20th Street NW
Suite 402
Washington, DC 20036
www.aafa.org

The Food Allergy & Anaphylaxis Network
10400 Eaton Place
Suite 107
Fairfax, VA 22030
www.foodallergy.org

Books

Baldwin, Carol. *Allergies*. Chicago: Heinemann, 2003.

Edelson, Edward. *Allergies*. Broomall, Penn: Chelsea House, 1999.

Peters, Celeste. *Allergies, Asthma, and Exercise: The Science of Health*. Chicago: Raintree, 2000.

Disclaimer
The website addresses (URLs) included in this book were valid at the time of going to press. However, because of the nature of the Internet, it is possible that some addresses may have changed or sites may have changed or closed down since publication. While the author and the publishers regret any inconvenience this may cause readers, no responsibility for any such changes can be accepted by either the author or the publishers.

Index